"I cannot heave my heart into my mouth..."

King Lear, Act 1, Scene 1

DANCING ON UNEVEN GROUND

BARBARA RAPHAEL

ESKOVA ENTERPRISES   VANCOUVER BC CANADA

ISBN: 978-0-9810065-2-9

Cover image: Shelby Miller
Author photo: Hannah Raphael

Eskova Enterprises Ltd.
www.eskovaenterprises.com

For Hannah, of course

CONTENTS

I

A Family's Heart
(For Hersch)

In the dread of a sleepless night
I pour words to paper,
Spill out my love for you,
Scribble your virtues,
Cheer your choices,
Laugh and weep for your tenderness
Wound tight like a spring bud.

In the grey of a rainy morning
I scrunch all sentiment, embarrassed
But needing you to know that I know
Who holds the heart of our family,
That without you,
We would disappear.

HANNAH

I bore you on my side sucking ice cubes in the night,
Screamed at the doctor,
Sent twelve yellow roses her way next day.

The old red brick building cradled us,
My arms swaddled you tight,
Deep inside the stiff white sheets.

I sang guardian angel tunes
To keep the whine of sirens from your perfect sleep,
Poked you to wake up.

Come play with me, I whispered.
You never let me down.

— BARBARA RAPHAEL —

LESSON

Far from shore and long ago
I swam your bare pink baby body
Out on the old blue air mattress,
Pushed you through the twinkling,
Blinked water from my eyes,
Watched you roll off without a sound,
Threads of golden hair like jellyfish tentacles
Casually disappearing into deep green shadow.

I dove, grabbed, sucked in salt,
Spluttered to the surface shocked.
You looked at me surprised,
Then laughed at the sun in your eyes
As my heart screamed like a wounded gull.

MOTHERHOOD

We moved when you were four
And wandered off.
I lost my breath til you ran back
From round the corner,
Not far, but far enough.
You puzzled at my wet face.

You're fifteen and I awake to raging rain
Pounding above my head,
Echoing my heartbeat,
Awaiting your tread on the stair
That always comes too late.

I groan at the ceiling
Wishing for the curfew I could never force,
Will myself to breathe,
Banish black pictures of you lying broken,
Drenched in a ditch
And all the will in the world cannot stop my stubborn hand
From reaching for the phone to summon your voice
To still my heart.
Just tell me you're alive, I whisper,

Weep into my pillow til I hear your steps
Below my mother-bed,
And sleep like a sedative releases me
Back to myself once more.

— BARBARA RAPHAEL —

TRACKING AUTUMN

A bumble bee busily dying on the window ledge
Wakes me with its buzzing.
I watch the morning sky
Turn leaves to black silhouettes.

I've been tracking autumn come
Colours on the mountainside,
Blurred greens and golds,
Walking the forest floor,
Crushing freshfall underfoot.

A leaf turned brittle, brown and shriveled
Spirals down onto my path
While one perfect bud on a bush,
Tight, taut and faintly pink,
Shivers like the nipple on a young girl's chest.

LIKE SHE ALWAYS DOES

She called to say she couldn't go,
To yet another appointment disappointed.
   Come over anyway we can have lunch at least,
Then sent me with a credit card to buy her favourite sandwich,
   Camembert and pear and whatever you want,
Whatever I wanted,
It was always so.

   I just try to stay in the moment, not think about it,
She says from her brown leather chair by the desk in the den,
But she talks about it anyway,
The pain,
As if she's done with it.

   Fix my shoes for me the closet's a mess,
   I only need one pair now,
Her swollen bandaged foot
Propped on the padded stool
Goes up and down up and down
Trying to find a way not to hurt,
That damn toe that would not heal.

We talk about people like we always do,
It's fun being wicked together,
Watch the afternoon shadows creep along the wall.

I say: *You know I'm going away, five weeks,*
She shrugs, I ask: *What's that look?* she says,
   I might not be here when you get back.
I ignore her: *It's only an operation, not even a general.*
She chuckles, *that's the good news,*
Clearly afraid.

— BARBARA RAPHAEL —

Her chin drops ever so slowly,
I get up to leave,
   So soon? she whines eyes closed
Wanting to prolong our visit,
Afraid she might miss something.
I bend down and she leans into me,
Like she always does,
Never giving her face her cheek her mouth,
Just lowers her head to receive my kiss,
A papal benediction.

I walk down the hall,
Cross the kitchen floor,
Let myself out,
Like I always do.

Last Sips

My auntie Mona died tonight
Just before midnight.

25 years ago I was at dinner at her place,
Her table her cooking,
When my waters broke
And two days later my baby girl slid out.

Tonight my daughter and Mona's daughter
And I say goodbye,
Altogether,
All to get her
To help her
Pass on
Pass over
Pass away.

My first death
I hold my breath
As her lips move in silence,
As a single teardrop slowly slides
Over her smooth unlined cheek.
Why are you crying? I wonder,

The breath is shallow now,
Like little fading sips,
No fighting
No clutching
No more rattling
Or as Hannah calls it, purring.
No more purring.

— Barbara Raphael —

I stroke her forehead,
Hannah holds her foot,
And Daya leans down, whispers
It's alright Mama, you can go now, it's safe.
I love you so much Mommy
It's okay
Goodbye Mommy
Goodbye Mommy
Goodbye Mommy.

We sit in wonder as Mona takes another sip,
Sighs, takes another,
Then one more.
And we wait
And we wait,
Holding our breath
For another, then another
As she sighs and rests
Then sips and stops.
And still we wait.

The room is full and dense,
It is important to move slowly,
Deliberately.
Hannah presses her throat for a pulse.

I begin to shiver,
The nurse comes in,
Listens for a heartbeat,
Nods and leaves.

Mona lies very still,
Becomes paler and paler as we watch
But still she is here.

Then Daya makes phone calls
As I turn to hug Hannah
And when I look again
Mona has gone.

We leave Daya alone with her mother,
Before the business of burying and grieving
And being gracious sets in.

We ride down the elevator in silence,
In awe that we were there to share
This moment together:
Auntie Mona's last tear
Last sigh
Last sip.

— BARBARA RAPHAEL —

Hospital Visit

Daddy's old now. It happened overnight.
A gap in his brain let some light leak out,
Leaving his hand unable to grip a pen,
His leg trailing behind like a hem too long.
Now he shuffles, wobbles, stoops.

Below his crumpled gown I glimpse
Hairless whiteness of well-shaped legs,
Look away as mother's hand lingers,
Absently stroking his familiar knee.

Outside the sun is setting,
The sky losing light goes gold,
Blends pink to darker blue.

Chocolate-bar wrappers litter the table
That hovers over his bed,
Others buried in the trash:
    Cadbury Caramilk
    Coffee Crisp
    O Henry!
I wonder who has eaten them,
Him or her?

She freshens his half of the room
To air out the roommate's reek,
Up from emerg today,
Found starving in an east side tenement
Too weak to reach the mission-meals around the block,
Found a bed instead beside my dad.
His farts fill the air my mother tries to spray away.

We talk about his book as the sun sets
Over a city he was young in once.

Oyster Sky and Brown Bananas

I
The narrow oyster sky,
Like wet blotting paper,
Ducks through my bedside window
Scuffed with specks of spiderweb.
Remnants of old spring pollen
Carve birdbone lines down its pane.

A goose down pillow props my head,
While drooping slants of rain lay tracks across my heavy lids,
The drizzle witness to my solitude.

Outside the cedar boughs droop,
Moss clumps cover trunks,
Branches bare at winter's edge,
Fog-grey in the downpour.

Field grass drowns in mud,
The pond rushes bow,
Its surface erupting into crown explosions,
The mountains mere memory behind soggy mists.

I nudge the window open,
Eavesdrop on the rain,
Beat and taps of bass and tympani,
Gurgling xylophonic trills,
An atonal symphony of silver drizzle and dumpling drops.

II
I excavate my feathered comfort
And ponder your hard bed,
Afar in the neon ward
Where you watch the Mariners get beaten again

— Barbara Raphael —

While above your head
Plastic tubes trail insolently
From your tendoned arm, your white bent back.

I know you refuse the insult of their food
Coaxed down by an angel nurse and Mom
Resting finally in a plastic chair pulled close to you.

On the window ledge visiting bananas turn brown.

Urology Ward

I've never seen my father's body
And now I've seen it all,
Will myself to look,
But still the world tilts.

Nothing gets through a blocked tube
Backup can pollute a hollow space
A drain, a straw, an ear
Impeded flow causes trouble
It ain't good…

A simple procedure botched,
Now nothing is easy for this frail old man
Slouching along the ward's dented floor,
One step at a time,
Spotted knuckles clutching the walker,
His aluminum life raft,
Til breathless back in bed
He sucks oxygen from a plastic hose
Stuck in his nose
As winter-hair flies white above his foggy face.

He swallows a plop of pale yellow egg,
Glares at the grey mushroom soup,
Bed clothes bunched as I watch
His gown slide slowly down his arm
Like yolk off a counter top,
Startled by his neck,
Naked without a perfect tie or paisley ascot.

The chair beside Dad's bed reclines for Mom
As they watch together, *Dancing with the Stars*
Til a little morphine eases him to sleep
And night takes her home to an empty bed.

— Barbara Raphael —

Ice Pick in My Foot

Dad has been moved
To a place where his brown leather chair won't fit,
Where there is no desk to write on,
And his narrow bed can't accommodate a wife.

I limp my way down the lino-grey floor,
Hallways littered with wheelchairs,
Avoid the scratching hands,
The crackled cries for help,
But I can never find him,
Only an unmade bed in a room he shares with a balding youth
Who never speaks, is often nude,
This forsaken place
Pulsing smells of mold and canned tomato soup.

When I see him and kneel down,
Take his gloved hand in mine,
I want to feel some measure of soft affection,
But pity pierces my foot like an ice pick,
Cold and blue like his eyes before they turned to water.

I watch a tear roll down his grizzled cheek.
Get me out of here! he pleads.
Each step screams as I take myself away.

Seat F56

My daddy died but I didn't cry,
Bought him a chair instead.
Not a beach bench or a pew,
But a seat in a tent we could look through.

My Father's Day gift, our tradition,
The plays we watched, our joy
Under red and white stripes:
> As the sun sets and the lights begin to twinkle;
> The long day wanes: the slow moon climbs.

We walked to the car cross dew drenched grass,
Held each other's arm for balance,
Reciting, analyzing, laughing,
Until one year - not long ago – he murmured…
I think this is it.

I did not cry, have not cried
For this big man set so high
Up on my childish pedestal
That eroded as I grew,
Dissolved to dust as I came to know him,
Was pointless later as I stooped to understand.

Grief is a mystery to me.
I felt more for little Bart,
The greying black terrier
I loved less than a year,
Or Sheila,
Who smoked herself to death even as I howled at her to stop.

So today I bought a seat - F56,
Where I will sit tomorrow and tomorrow and tomorrow,
And watch those poor players
Strut and fret their hour upon the stage.

It seems grief will not be full of sound and fury,
But a soft, sweet song between us.

— Barbara Raphael —

WHERE'S DADDY?

Driving was her lifeline,
Sustained her through the world she knew,
Even as she clung to its edges,
Pedal to the floor.

While old friends sickened or died,
She shopped for gifts,
Helped out, took meals, consoled,
Carrying her affections in the car
To a world where age was just a state of mind.
Still, they took her car away.

She lived with a cranky old man,
Who stumbled around in the night to pee,
Growled at her for more or hotter,
Shut the window I'm cold!
And she hopped as she had to his tyrant bark
For all their seventy years.

But she still could go out,
Buy his strawberry ice cream,
Food for dinners she barely cooked anymore,
Could drive him to appointments, herself to bridge,
A lunch with the girls now and then,
An outing just for fun.

She wrote the cheques, paid the bills, carried credit cards,
Knew the balance in her bank account
Until they took all that away too.
She's getting old, it's practical, they said.

I can still drive, she cried,
But her boys laughed
And she didn't know how to fight,

But I did.
Retested, twice she passed, drove again, rear-ended a car.
See? they said, *This is your fault!*

She tried taxis, couldn't fathom the bus,
Stayed home,
Grew stiff and cloudy.
He's too much for her, they said,
She needs a rest,
But knit together by the years,
Apart they unraveled to wrinkled ruin.

She lost her home, her husband, then her mind,
Tore once perfect nails til her fingertips bled,
Slept a lot,
Forgot her earrings, then her lipstick,
Reassured us with her smile that she was fine,
But her eyes weren't in it.

Where's Daddy? she asked.

— BARBARA RAPHAEL —

HIDDEN CHOCOLATE

The light in my mother's eyes paled,
Her mind cracked like pond ice
And now I wonder what she sees
Staring into those depths.

Memories slip away one word at a time,
Tease and tickle
Like a fly that lands for just one breath
And then is gone.

But she can sing all the words to *My Funny Valentine*,
Propping up her stooped man
Shuffling one foot to find the other.
Sixty-eight years they tripped fantastic,
And in her heart she dances still,
And prowls in the night for hidden chocolate.

I Dreamed I was Set Upon by Hooligans

I
Matching camel hair skirts and sweaters,
A closet full of multi-hued shoes and leather gloves,
Sweating in the cedar-lined sauna,
This was my life.

Mom's ivory white Mercedes,
Dad's cool grey Jag,
The monstrous midnight-blue Bentley
I learned to drive on
Shimmer in the shadows
Forever clean.
Our white-uniformed maid
Living in some room I never entered,
A tinkling bell at the dinner table
To summon her servitude,
This was my life.

Rhododendron in pink purple white
Rolled down the flower'd driveway,
Hugged our brown and white Tudor house.
Seven bathrooms, two sets of stairs,
Weekly gardeners and a security man
Who watched in the night
Ignoring the boy who hung from the ledge
Of my bedroom window,
Dropping to the grass below.
This was my life.

Fresh squeezed morning orange juice,
Clean sheets at night,
Those Saturday nights
When macaroni and cheese was our treat,
The nights the parents went out,

— Barbara Raphael —

When all those white table-cloth'd dinners
Of roasts of beef, chops of pork, legs of lamb, sides of salmon
Took a rest.

Caterers and florists and bartenders
Regularly readied the house,
Filled it up with food and flowers,
Packed polished sterling bowls with chocolates
We bit into looking for the caramels,
And pilfered pastries from the pantry,
Pop from the fridge.
Me and my brothers peeped down though the railings,
As Mother's party laugh and Father's pipe smoke
Swirled up to comfort us,
Past bedtime
Past midnight
Past childhood.
I'd curl into my parent's bed,
Breathing deep as if asleep,
Hoping for a conversation that mentioned my name.

And in the later years,
Dressing for my entrance down the long thick staircase
Where waiting party-goers
Motioned with their drinks and cocktail napkins,
As servers in black and white
Wove their silent way through crowded rooms.

Into the party hum I pranced,
Flowers and cigarette butts overflowing their bowls,
And the many-leaved dining room table groaned,
Burdened with bitesize sandwiches,
Splayed with sliced honeyed hams, carved barons of beef,
Pickles and horseradish and mustards waiting to adorn.
Radishes cut like red and white tulips,
Carrots curled into orange wheels,
Asparagus speared and standing true

Reflected in the glow of silver bowls trays platters,
Dishes rimmed in gleaming gold, lapis blue.

I knew my place in this world
Without guile
Without guilt
Without a doubt
That this would ever end.

Then it was gone,
And the golden pillow that cushioned me and broke my falls,
Slit open, spilled out feathers
That floated far away.
Like a child whose balloon has popped,
I was left startled and dismayed.

II
I dreamed I was standing outside a red Cadillac
Made dusty on some old dirt road
In the middle of a nowhere I'd ever been
And stubble-chinned men hunched towards me
With dirty fingernails and ragged hair,
Their red and black checked jackets stained and open
I at their mercy had nowhere to run,
No one to hear my cries for help
From their fierce eyes blind to me
Tugging at the doors of the big red car
That stayed forever closed.

When I awoke I had a child,
No Visa card to help us out.
No one got it,
And those that did, I guessed,
Thought comeuppance and fled.

It was okay though,
I didn't get it either.

— BARBARA RAPHAEL —

SHORN

I came upon a zip lock bag and held it up,
Looked in at mother-daughter locks,
One black silver-laced braid,
A carefree pony tail,
Unattached, unnatural.

Touch them she said, but
Singed I turned away,
Harkening back to summer camp,
The films I had to watch,
Black and white and grainy,
Filmed in hurried horror of the other camps,
Where abandoned eyeglasses piled high as African ant-hills,
Bent heaps of empty suitcases,
Mounds of glaring gold meant for melting
Wept beside the furnace fire.

Mini mountains of child ringlets,
Father and brother *peyus,*
Mother-dense braids,
Stacked in disbelieving dunes,
Innocent curls incinerated,
Lost like disappearing tendrils
To our forgetting.

This blameless hair preserved in plastic,
Rich with indifference,
Immune to memory,
Destined for another's shaved head.

Shorn of words I say nothing.

Mother Dance

Fierce is a mother facing gale force grief,
Leaning into it,
Shoulders back,
Ready for the next blow.

She insists her rage,
Matching nature's might
Scream for howling scream,
Face like some desert landing strip
Strafed with scars of a daughter lost.

Thumb out by the side of a Sudbury highway,
Homeward bound from her cross-country quest,
The girl was hit by a boy
Driving his new red pick-up truck,
Both twenty, one dead.
The youth slipped away while his father's man
Slit her open for signs of sins. Organs intact,
The boy awoke next morning with a mighty hangover,
As the mother searched the ditch
For remnants of her tattered child.

She stomps her laced up boots upon the high-school stage,
We can't turn away,
Watch stunned,
As she raises her fists in the air
And we rise to stomp with her,
Joining in her mother dance,
A beastly, primal reckoning.

Bathed in light she speaks the words
That give her to us one last time,
Sliding from image to image,
Insisting we know who she was.

This is not a celebration!

— Barbara Raphael —

2

for Sheila

THURSDAY NEWS

It's nothing real,
This unraveling.
The threads cannot contain the moment.
      Come sit she says,
      I have something to tell you
And we assemble,
Wine glass in hand.

The air is still
And life stops, suddenly.
Buzzing and twitterings,
The neighbour's voice,
A sprinkler's hiss
Suspended in the sunlight
As we three old friends sip our wine,
As she speaks the words
That change our lives forever.

The wall of words,
Like distant thunderclaps,
The wall we slam into
That takes our breath away,
Raindrops of lead that hurt our hearts,
And we know,
Even as we will not admit we know,
That this is the first day
Of a long journey.

CHEMO WEDNESDAY

Chemo day is Wednesday,
Not for the weak of heart.

Up elevators they trail
Into that room indifferent
To race colour gender age,
Sexual persuasion.
Here all veins are equal
To the probing needle,
The nurse's patient touch.

Hope does not discriminate
This multicultural ragtag band
Swinging through the doorway
For their fix.

The doctors make no promises,
No money back guarantees,
Play the odds:
     50/50
     65/35
What do you have to lose?

The answer so final,
Forces them through the doors,
Sets them on their stubborn seats,
Demands the will that drags them back
Each Wednesday,
Each chemo Wednesday.

— BARBARA RAPHAEL —

A Good Day Along the Drive

Aram hot-compressed the wound,
Wringing out water,
Rising steam from the silver bowl
That made her back so red.

Drove down to the Drive,
To the Co-op for milk, lemons, yogurt,
  We're out of butter?
  Where did all the butter go?
  Gone to green beans every one…
As we ate beets from the container,
Sitting round the kitchen table,
Fingers turning red.

Back on the Drive we laughed,
Reading wicked cards in the shop,
Agreed we could send them only to each other.
  You've got not to mind
  Someone seeing your shit
  So clear so well.
So dear you are to me.

Tired we sat,
Drank coffee in red chairs by a window,
As *She* tried to make sense
Of matters of the heart.

When Liz came upon us
We perched on the peeling bus-stop bench
Marveling at the mysteries of willful puberty
And the miracles we carry inside.

KEMOSABE DAY

First floor reception,
She bustles in late.
Up to the second floor,
This fateful place
That hums with the silence of waiting.

Like bored travelers in a bus station,
Back to back they sit.
So many, she moans, so many,
And turns her face away,
Toward her gatekeepers,
The keepers of her gate
At her side
To keep away
To keep at bay.

She fills out forms,
Imbibes information,
Is ushered into a tiny white room with no chairs.
We stand, her gatekeepers.

She tells her story - again,
Eloquent and graceful
To this doctor dressed like an airline hostess,
Tight polite,
Who utters the word (how dare she!) …
Chemotherapy.

Keee…Mo…Thair…Uppee…
Kee…Mo…Saab…Bee…
Kemosabe!

— BARBARA RAPHAEL —

The gatekeepers her Tontos,
She, our Lone Ranger
Courageously fighting the forces of evil!

Her Tontos attend intently:
  12 weeks, 4 rounds, 3 months.
The Lone Ranger nods.
Oh, she sighs, I get to keep my hair
And pot alleviates the nausea.
Maybe we can get our hands on some,
(Muted chuckles),

Hi Ho Silver,
Awaaaaay!!

THE SOUND OF DYING

Outside:
In the garden,
Bird-cheeps and twitters.
The wind this grey chilly Saturday
Rustles the grapevine leaves.

Clematis tendrils sweep the pane,
A distant dog yaps,
A crow calls a buzzing bee,
A motorbike clears its throat,
Vague muted traffic ticks.

Kai is restless,
Pokes his head into the daisy patch,
Circles the cement,
Lies down to lick his balls,
Stiff collar clinking
For Sheila's ears
Above.

Inside:
We have no words
For this day of death rattlings.
Rattles are for babies, I protest.
I think this calls for chocolate, says Christine.
Lucille murmurs low on the phone to Bev,

We got suits yesterday, Lucas tells Barbi,
Expensive, expensive, expensive, he laughs.
I really like the socks,
Very pink,
Very silk
Why not, says Lucille,
They're kind of Sheila-ish.

— BARBARA RAPHAEL —

We chuckle,
Standing around inside the kitchen.
Aram says: I'd rather buy a car.
Dom says: The suit will last longer.

Christine and Martha go off to the store,
Lucille makes her Caesar dressing,
Barbie walks up the stairs,
Aram's head is in the fridge,
Barbara scribbles at the table.

The sound of dying is like no other.

THE SHAPE OF GRIEF

Grief is not a wail or a flood,
Demands nothing
But that you pay it some attention
Once in a while.

Grief does not insist itself,
Awaits its moment patiently,
Hovering like the loon in a tree
That ruffles its feathers, snoozes,
Then soars.

Grief is an ache that comes and goes,
Swamped at first,
Slamming inside and the words are still
I can't believe she's gone.

Grief lives in night's dreams,
Doles out glimpses of the beloved,
Soothing, tantalizing, teasing.

She wafts through dreams,
Laughs in the store where we read funny cards,
Plays with Kai on the Spanish Banks sand flats,
Buys her special yogurt on The Drive,
Bustles in her kitchen,
Lies on Lucille's couch,
Adores the trees and rocks on Valdez,
Scolds my eating habits,
Bemoans my cough
And tells me in no uncertain terms
It's time for a haircut.

— BARBARA RAPHAEL —

She arrives late for family dinners,
Sits by my side in the cinema eating popcorn with butter,
Calls me to see how my day has gone
And to tell me the latest secret
She's not supposed to tell.

She is with me when I sleep and when I wake
In the ocean when I swim
In the forest where I walk
In my arms telling me she loves me.

The shape of grief is that it has no shape.

TIME'S MAGIC

If you saw me sipping tea in your living room,
Playing tag with your son,
Clearing the clutter from the dinner we ate,
Laughed gossiped drank,
What would you think?

If you saw me walking down the street,
Scooping shells off the beach,
Reading at some pock-marked table over coffee in a Kits cafe,
Chatting on the phone,
Eating my blueberry scone...

If you saw me buying a toothbrush, newspaper, loaf of bread
Some busy Friday afternoon,
Or sitting on a bench in the night
That tingles with frost and blooms...

Would you know my dreams were filled with impossible reunions
Painted gold and far away?
Would you know my mornings were reluctant,
Peeked through careful curtains that shut out the light?

Would you see the candle flickering in its lotus nest
On the old oak table where your picture rests
Beside the green stone Buddha,
The tall turquoise vase
Watering whatever rose iris lily
I bought that week?

I dial the number that has no ring
Before the thought she won't pick up
Comes whooshing like an avalanche,

— BARBARA RAPHAEL —

Whips my breath away,
Leaves me cold.

Look into my eyes and ask me
If time heals all,
And I will whisper not yet,
Not yet.

I Never Knew

I never knew grief could be so exhausting,
The work of it
The weight of it
The early morning wakings
To yet another day.

It is absence like an abyss,
Angling for advantage,
Mumbling in my ear,
Not words but moans.

It is the smile that startles me in photographs,
Propped against the vase by my kitchen window,
By the vitamin bottle in the bathroom,
As I brush my teeth,
Morning time, night time,
And no part of me swallows this!

No one so big gets to disappear like that,
And I will rage against it into all these good nights,
The sleepless nights,
The missings.

I never knew grief could be so exhausting!

— Barbara Raphael —

SUBTLE

I thought grief was a loud howling sound
Taking up the space inside
Demanding attention
Cymbals clashing, cellos groaning
Full of sound and fury.

I thought grief meant crying buckets of tears,
Mascara running through eyes puffed shut,
Piles of soggy tissues on the floor

I thought grief was communal,
One big group hug,
Getting lost in some collective comforting,
An enduring embrace.

But grief is more subtle than that.
It's the shift in appetite,
The taste for food diminished,
The sudden nausea nudging me back.

It is the deepest of remembering,
Like a movie in my head,
Full technicolour, sense-surround,
Replaying every vivid detail,

And so, so alive!

A WALK WITH YOU

Up the hill thick with fallen leaves,
Above the beach,
I walk in the rain
And in my heart you are with me,
Chattering and huffing,
Sucking in the autumn,
Arms flung wide,
Head back laughing,
Hear you say,
Oh, I love this!

I stop at the rotting wooden railing
Where you took my picture
As I stretched my unused muscles,
Where you lit up a smoke,
Knowing I'd hate it.

We crunched through the undergrowth,
Lifted our feet around tripping roots,
Fleshed out fantasies:
A coffee-bar-art-gallery!
Mexico and a tavern on the beach!
We can do anything! you shouted.
A woman of property, I laughed.
I am so full up! echoed down the canyon.

When Kai bounced off you called him back
With that big bark of yours,
A foghorn blast that startled me,
So big a sound from your small body.

My face is wet with these phantom sounds,
As I slip down to the empty car below.

— BARBARA RAPHAEL —

One Year

We built a bonfire on the rocks,
Unearthed old marshmallows,
Scrounged kosher hotdogs from Saul and Sharon,
Sharpened green alder branches,
Watched the sky give in to shades
Of pink and gold and orange,
Magenta, purple,
An impossible sunset!

The darkest blue of indigo
Held the moon's neon beam
In honour of this night.
The air still seaweed-cedar fragrant
Smooth sandstone cradling our bums
As we ate and drank wine
And remembered.

Across the ocean where the city lives,
Fireworks snapped to attention as if on cue,
The Festival of Lights flung its display our way,
Silently spraying sparks across the water,
No match for the moon.

We toasted her and missed her.
No tears, no speeches,
Just absence.

3

SINGING HIS BREAKFAST

He wakes singing songs of his own making,
Nonsense words spun into tunes,
A domestic mantra,
Repeated over and over.
Deep in the drifts of sleep,
I dig my way to consciousness,
While winter morning traces
Smoky strobes of lingering night.

I eavesdrop on his slippered steps
Crossing the icy floor,
Down dusty brick red stairs
To the black iron wood stove
That sheds ash like dandruff on an old man's back,
Yawns open to catch the logs.

Encased in white down,
Only my nose feels the chill.

He makes his breakfast every day:
   Two cups of milk tea,
   Poached eggs and spinach,
   Tomatoes and toast,
Eats from the deep tangerine bowl,
Reading the screen for news of the world,
The weather, his British sports.

He gently shuts my bedroom door, I sigh,
Bury my face in the covers.
All's well in the world if Eddie is singing his breakfast.

RECENTLY I HAVE BEGUN TO THINK ABOUT SPIDERS
(For Stella)

Recently I have begun to think about spiders
The scariest bug of all,
Eight legs horrify,
Really just the world's finest tiny game hunters.

Carnivores,
Insects their meat of choice,
Entire lives spent hunting and devouring other bugs -
Flies bedbugs gypsy moths cockroaches grasshoppers
Even bees…
The real exterminators.

Spider silk stronger than tensile steel,
Crosshairs in optical instruments, gun sights,
Folk remedy to clot the blood.

Most spiders live in solitude,
Nocturnal hunters,
Their jaws too weak to break human skin.
No need to be afraid,
They prefer a tranquil existence,
Run away shy,
Try to hide
To be left alone to hunt,
Can't even see well,
Can hardly walk on flat surfaces,
Hang out in their webs.

I stomp my feet, shake out the bed clothes and make a pact:
I won't disturb your hunting if you stay out of my bed!

— BARBARA RAPHAEL —

Rapunzel's Revenge

When I was young I dreamed of swamps
Where thick muck held my feet.

Awake, I dreaded
The stickiness of everyday life.

The palace I lived in was plush,
Soft muted tones of rust and beige,
Jade green and autumn orange,
Full of familiar routines that lulled me to sleep.

Everything had its perfect place, everyone too,
Propped up by propriety,
While I was mired in mud no one could see.

Sometimes at night I would escape and drive,
The fancy car clung to curves like a slalom skier.

When I finally shimmied down from the tower,
I cut my hair, got a chocolate lab, and never wore shoes again.

FRECKLES

She came screaming into a crooked world
Stuck with thorns she could not fathom,
Kept plucking them out of her tenderness,
A prickly path she picked her way through.

No moon-face dolls and gingham,
No pinks or giggles in the night,
Just baseball caps and biceps,
The dependable pal, all zipped up
Lest secrets sewn into seams come undone.

Til love hit her one day,
And life unrolled the crimson carpet
That they soared down
While flashbulbs popped
And she laughed love into their light!

She gloried in the smoothness of her new rose-petal life.
The thorn pricks healed,
And little dobs, like freckles,
Were all that was left.

— BARBARA RAPHAEL —

PASLEY ISLAND
(for Col and Bud)

We were young there once
Exalting in our strength,
Climbed and dove, lay naked on the rocks,
Slipped on sodden mosses,
Bathed all day in the bay.

We knew where the secrets hid,
In dusty oak drawers
Hastily shoved, forgotten in darkness.
Some we uncovered midst giggles and gasps,
Others dissolved from neglect.

The ancient cedar grew through the deck,
Shaded us, watched us
Bounce down misshapen rocks
To the beach pebbled in pale greens and shiny blacks,
Star whites, pinks and sooty greys,
Smooth enough to cradle us
Where we sat and laughed,
Schemed and dreamed,
Dared and shared,
Laughed fearlessly.

The loft bed, the bunk bed, the princess bed, the tent bed,
I knew them all.
Magazines molding in the outhouse,
Musty canvas and kerosene lamps,
Smoke of green mosquito coils at night
Mingled with burning logs in the big stone fireplace,
A sweet, fine net that overlaid our senses.

How many feasts we had!
Each kitchen iteration where we cooked,
Embraced the rituals of planning and shopping,
Loading and unloading,
Into and out of whatever boat was going at the time.
Everyone chopped and tasted and salted,
Sipped good wine and sang along,
Peeled and sautéed,
Roasting, grilling, laughing.
No one was idle.

Under the stars we ate,
Crammed thigh to thigh at the long picnic table,
Elbows competing for room,
Til candles lit and glasses filled,
We piled our mismatched plates,
Savoured our creations,
Toasted the occasions,
Beside the flickering lamps,
Year after year

Wrapped in timeless patched blankets,
Sat deep in paint-chipped Adirondacks
We sipped more wine (or even better, scotch),
Watching the gentle bay reflect
The dinner lights, the neighbour lights, the stars
So safe, so sure,
In that Pasley Island place,
The container for our friendship,
Our children,
Our rememberings,
Our secrets.

— BARBARA RAPHAEL —

Heron

He ducks and bows and with each step
The heron stretches long his neck,
A cool grey curve uncoiling skyward,
Inching along the water's edge.

Casual wader he waits one-eyed,
Tilting at the sky, the sea,
Watching me I like to think,
But in one blink, one careless breath
I miss his move,
He's speared the flat white-bellied prey
Now trapped between his scissor-beak.

The slightest shake shows fish-life caught,
Now lodged within that bended arc,
Its darkened course through crooked craw
Distorting all that elegance.

Heron swallows from the shallow tide
To help fish on its way,
While I walk on to find mine.

Visit to the Art Gallery

I watched him from the sweaty bed
Through the open bathroom door
In the red and white cottage on the beach
Where he had come to visit.
Sliding my hand along the length of him I thought,
I know this man's body better than my own,
Sure even then that the memory of him
Would be all I could keep.

I pay my $12.50,
Pass through the new Chagall,
Climb the graceful staircase to the Smithson exhibit,
Where he waits.

Black and white photographs patch walls I walk past,
Slow as a sleepwalker to the alcove at the end of the room
Where three opaque plastic chairs wait side by side.

I pull the middle one up close
To the screen I cannot touch,
Take a breath and there he is.

I suck him in as he begins to talk,
Words ringing silent in my ears,
I know those elbowed threads
Hanging from the hole in his denim shirt,
That navy vest he hangs his finger on,
Those faded jeans over lean-long thighs.

I watch him push metal-framed glasses up the bridge of his nose
With those long fingers I knew so well
That loved to tap rhythms on any surface at hand,
The familiar typewriter he beat two-fingered,
Composing letters to me that I burned rashly
Before I knew three decades
Between loving and forgetting
Is a very long time.

— Barbara Raphael —

Storm Bay

The bird sailed by,
Returned, hovered, swooped,
Staying in the window of our gaze.
Strange flight for a heron, he said.

Its creaking caw called to us,
Breaking the dusk-silence.
It's Jess, I whisper,
And off it flew.

The eagle has been at work in the Bay,
Said Flakey in the morning,
Most chicks didn't make it,
The goslings, mergansers;
No herons for a couple of years, he shook his head,
A shame.

Later, silhouetted against the purple sky
At the end of Brian's rolling wall
Half deep in high tide,
A merganser and her one baby chick
Snuggle close.

HORSE

Horror on Hastings,
Littered with the homeless,
Their drive-by sidewalks.

A girl on the curb jerks like a puppet
To her unstrung song,
Jaws working its sideways dance,
Eyes jitterbugging white in their sockets,
Jean skirt tight as a sausage skin,
Laceless sneakers scuffed,
Scraped grey as her scaly knees.
Up a littered lane I turn,
Where hooded figures exchanging street currencies
Hunched smoking by a broken stone wall,
Glance my way,
I lock the doors,
Reverse.

That night visited by horses
Writhing on a dusty road,
Mouths like crimson caverns
Wild eyes white,
Stampeding into a perilous pile,
Too big, too dangerous to approach,
I am helpless.

The hill above is littered with their bodies,
Still and black against a metallic sky.
Others frantic charge,
And I know they will kill me if they can.
I run for cover,
Away from the madness.

— BARBARA RAPHAEL —

RAINDROPS ON BAMBOO

Raindrops on bamboo
Wash away the dust,
Bend stiletto leaves
To their insistent will.

The line-up is long today,
Puddles deep by the curb.
A young woman stands beside me,
Huddled around herself,
Unprotected against the downpour,
Getting soaked without a coat,
One thin, pink sweater over her white blouse.

I edge closer,
Move my umbrella slowly
Over her bowed head,
Hoping she doesn't notice,
Not wanting to give offense.

The taxis come,
No one speaks or jostles or taps their feet.
She glances at me,
Seems to shrug, doesn't move away,
She doesn't wish to give offense either.
Rain falls steadily, heavily, steaming the streets.

My shoes are soaked,
Tan pant legs turn dark brown,
Slip down my hips,
While rain drips off my umbrella
Rivulets down my right side.
I shift my purse.

I know the drops are soaking her too,
Her left side,
But we are locked in place,
Neither nodding to this soggy sharing.

Polite and motionless we stand,
Our exposed sides getting wetter and wetter,
I want to say something,
Share our predicament, laugh
But she is still,
And I'm not sure she'd understand me anyway.
I'd wipe the rain and sweat off my face,
But dare not, for fear of knocking more water onto her.

Finally she is next in line,
Steps in a puddle, gets into the taxi, closes the door
Still not looking at me as she pulls away
And I'm left wondering, once again,
If I'd caused offence.

When I arrive at school
Soaked pants dragging,
Arms and right side drenched,
The secretaries in the office only smile and shrug.
I walk up the three flights to the staff room
(Elevator for heavy transport only),
Sliding my hand up the wet metal railing,
Where my colleagues laugh good-naturedly,
Hand me a tissue to dry myself.

A sarong in my bag becomes the day's skirt.
Rebecca takes my pants down to the dryer.
She does this quietly,
Not wishing to give offense.

— BARBARA RAPHAEL —

TYPHOON YORK

2:30 a.m. and a movie plays,
Black and white on a little screen,
Me and Gary Cooper
Waiting for this galloping storm.

On the 22nd floor I'm being rocked
Inside a giant cradle whose bough could break
And tumble me down,
No sleep for this baby.

They raised the signal from 8 to 10!

Swaying like an eagle in its nest,
Atop a tree in my B.C. rainforest,
No one is home when I call,
But here the China Sea bangs below.

Bathroom door swings on its hinges,
Beaded strands on its handle rattle,
Hanging utensils twist and turn in the kitchen.
I wish someone would answer!

Rain rampages by my window,
Streaked with beads of jittering water,
Like on a jet plane ascending,
Or the dry cycle in a car wash.

The wind wants in,
Shrill as a half-time whistle,
Paws like a howling wolf,
Furious at 150 mph.

Seasick I clutch my pillow,
Knees to chest,
Listen to the screams.

Pick up, pick up!

HOMESICK

The water looks inviting from the thirty-second floor,
Blue sky and hazy mountains to the east,
Airport bridge as clear as the Lions Gate back home.
To the north China hulks,
My Hong Kong home.
On the street thick air steams,
Bright red meat drips blood and flies,
Yellow star fruit, tiny bananas, soft mangoes
Ooze juices and clog my nostrils,
Sturdy pink handkerchief catches my sweat.

Air conditioners long overdue for a filter change
Deal some relief.
I sprint from building to taxi to underground train
That spits me into one more indifferent mall,
Trying to avoid the heat, the constant crowds
That clamour me to tears.

I dream of tall green cedar trees
Overhanging cold ocean summer swims,
Of tea with friends at our local café,
Count the sleeps til I am home.

— BARBARA RAPHAEL —

I'M STILL HERE

("I was still in here – I was still me..." Jill Bolte Taylor)

Last night I dreamed I took three steps and fell
To the wooden floor outside my room
On to my face, lay still, unhurt
But cold upon the hardness.

Before in bed arms numb,
Right index finger dead asleep,
Leg muscles twitching, undulating
As if tiny alien creatures
Lived just under the surface of my skin,
I wanted to come
And curl myself around you.

The bumping woke you up.
I heard your bare feet coming,
Slapping the wood in the dark,
Lit by the light of the stove's clock.

Eyes open, rigid as the frozen floor,
My flimsy white t-shirt struggling to protect,
I was laughing, felt silly, unhurt,
But you couldn't know, or hear me,
Saw only this quiet face upon the floor.

I watched your face fill with fear.
Look into my eyes, I chide,
I'm still here!

When I awoke, night air on my face,
I looked outside my room
To see if I was there.

Deep in the Bone

Deep in the bone where no fingers reach
I seek relief,
While nerves inside insist
Wake up! I am not done with you.

This body turns and twists,
Huddled naked knees and ankles
Sandwich one long pillow
Easing flesh on flesh,
While green-eyed hours stare me down.

My mind embroiders dreams with throbbings
That seep through and overlaps to waking,
Screams,
I am not done with you!

— Barbara Raphael —

PRETENDING

A new hip he said
And thanking him I clicked my heels,
Phoned my friends then spent
Fell into bed beside myself.

Who knew walking the seawall was such a luxury,
Or squatting to clear winter leaves from sprouting tulips
Meant needing a hand up?

I will watch those hands
Put visiting dahlias in my vase,
Rummage round my fridge for chicken soup,
Smell my private perfumes
Huddled on the glass shelf above the toilet
Now raised to please the angle
My new hip must sit upon.

Everyone has a story
To help me be less afraid.
I pretend I'm not.

Neurosurgery

They cut into my spinal column,
Fused my neck,
Played around so very close
To the place where my brain peeks out.
I feel it in my feet,
The slightest touch burns.

Hunched and hobbling I laugh in the mirror,
Take one step at a time,
Place, step, down, repeat,
Weak disembodied legs,
Down the stairs,
Hugging the rail,
Trailing my hand for balance.

A hot sudsy bath,
Lights low, lavender drops,
I float in the breath, submerged,
Focus on my feet feeling lighter, softer
The soothing sensation of water.

Denial does not rescue me
Like all the times before,
When I would wake and walk,
When this body forgave my sins.
I was so certain it would rise again,
And now I need a stick to walk.

If I could live inside each moment,
Each movement,
Would I be less afraid?

— Barbara Raphael —

EVEREST

When forced to stop I'm still surprised,
Take off my jeans get into bed,
Lie on my side and watch
The chickadees and red-breast finch
Compete for space on the green plastic feeder
Plastered to the window,
Littered with specks of sunflower seeds and droppings.

This tired is a gnawing burden,
A heavy pack that turns the stairs into an Everest trek,
Each step a boulder, dragged behind.

Summit reached,
Kindness and Patience wrap their arms around me,
Guide me gently to bed,
Turn off the phone,
Pull up the covers and whisper,
Rest.

Dancing Fool

She sits by a window frosted into patterns of despair,
Wrapped in mohair memories,
Memorizing lines from Shakespeare,
The great love play's Prologue
That begs forgiveness before it begins.

Once she mocked all careful cries,
Lay on a ship's wooden railing
That spanned the Indian Ocean,
Sped between crooked coconut palms,
Spun out on sandy jungle paths,
Perched on the edge of sacred cliffs where eagles float,
Dangled booted feet into nothingness.

But fearlessness like dampened flames
Dissolved to disappointed dust
As her body ate her spirit,
And when she woke into her life,
Dancing was beyond her,
And only the fool remained,
Dragging a foot down lost trails of glory.

— Barbara Raphael —

SKOOKUMCHUCK TRAIL

White mushrooms embrace broken cedar stumps,
Red and yellow leaves give under our hiking boots,
Westcoast giant ferns stroke the path,
Moss hangs like abandoned fishing nets
Dripping their green from towering branches
Of giant Douglas fir and hemlock,
Doing their best to keep us dry.

The thunder-grey clouds move quickly
As rainfall echoes back and forth,
Flattens under our footfall,
Drop, drip, drop and whispering shush
Make puddles to splash through.

Today I walk the Skookumchuk trail,
A soggy triumph.

At the end of the trail I rest,
Bum perch on a shiny boulder,
Peer down through the chain link fence
At the roaring chuck that sucks
Whatever floats into its maw,
Fatal to those who don't know it.

We backtrack into the forest,
Rain coming heavy now,
Pick up our pace,
My poles like a trusty dog
Sniffing out snaggle roots for me to step over.

I marvel that I have no pain.

Happy Birthday!

My bum has recently fallen,
Rests on the back of crinkled thighs,
Mottled and white like birch bark,
Shins shriveled to shapeless posts,
Red bulging bunions
Bullied into sensible shoes,
Breasts like the paps of some Amazonian
Stirring clay pots in the jungle.

Age is a creeper vine
Winding round memory,
Climbing like a socialite
In a brown-edged gown.

Halting along the sidewalk,
Reflected in the glass,
I am weak with recognition,
Like a word confounded,
This familiar woman
Whispers my name to the night.

— Barbara Raphael —

GULLS

Searching the seas for impossible answers
I watch the gulls,
Their bobbing dance along the shore,
Foam and feathers poking at alabaster shells.

Black wing-tipped white-bellied,
Crying their longing to the sea,
Like a famished fisherwife
Despairing of her drowning prayers.

They swoop down gull-grey,
Rise like a veil over indigo waves,
Merging with the clouds.

Placid now,
A wrinkled calm,
Like me.

FORGOTTEN

Shadows of prayers cough in corners,
Captive in ancient spider webs,
Pale secrets keep them company,
Shrouded by the dusk.

In the childhood cellar where the toybox lived,
Spilling dress-up gowns and costume glitter,
High heeled shoes to play pretend,
Solitary tea parties kept her company
On rainy Saturday afternoons.

When she had her own house,
The prayers slumbered,
Packed in an old cracked trunk
Jammed with keepsakes no one would ever see.

One day she stooped to call them to her,
Caught a hem, lost her balance,
And then those prayers,
Like fireflies illuminating promises,
Lost their light,
And falling she forgot
What she had ever dreamed
For herself.

— BARBARA RAPHAEL —

THE GIFT

Wisdom defines age not years
Does not come and go like fashion fads or daffodils
Is worn like a modest shawl that needs no drama.

Shared with those who can listen
Have lived to suffer life's barbs and arrows
Endured the big and little times
That can destroy a soul.

Wisdom is the gift earned at the end of a journey
You never imagined you'd take
Within the unknown where the lessons sleep
Waiting for you to waken to whisper
You are not alone.

DANCING ON UNEVEN GROUND

Missed the food but found a seat,
Next to the dessert table
Groaning under Esther and Uli's
Handmade chocolate treats.

A million small children bounced and rolled
In front of the stage on bumpy ground.
Dads held babies, moms fed them,
The pretty boom-boom boys set up.

Speeches of history and gratitude,
The 2 matriarchs still standing,
Serene in their 90's,
Smiling their secrets and speaking their stories,
Strong in wit and wisdom.

The Slugs pounded back the beat,
Forcing old and cripples to their feet.
Ditched my sticks,
Any steady shoulder would do,
Shook free my hair - and danced!

The stars came out,
And still they stomped the grass,
Flung children in the air,
Til one by one they dropped
To sleep upstairs on papa's chest,
Or here and there in Kendall nooks and crannies.

I lay my hand on Sarah's heart,
She covered mine with hers,
I said goodbye,
Bent down to kiss her cheek,
Then hobbled to my car,
Len and Lizzie my support.

We're all dancing on uneven ground.

— BARBARA RAPHAEL —

ACKNOWLEDGEMENTS

I wish to thank all who have encouraged me in this endeavour. To Leonard who makes me walk 'just to the next bench'. To The *Rubies* who bear witness. To Gillian and Richard who love me even when I say no. To Marlena who asked and listened. To Carol and her sublime relationship with words who put this book together. To my soulmate, Eddie, who supports me just by being Eddie. And to my heartmate, Ann, who in so many ways made this book possible.

To my community of friends too numerous to mention who over the years have loved and sustained me, I am everlastingly grateful.

And, finally to the children, Stella, Simone, Wesley, and now Gray, who bring me joy and feed my soul.

About the Author

Barbara Raphael has been writing in one form or another for as long as she can remember. *Dancing on Uneven Ground* is her first collection of poems.

She was born in Vancouver, and despite having traveled the world lives there still, dividing her time between the city and the Sunshine Coast.

For many years Barbara was a counsellor and an educator. Now, as a Life-Cycle Celebrant, she combines her collective talents to create unique ceremonies for life's many passages.

She is fortunate in her community of friends, and values them beyond all else.

She loves dogs but doesn't have one.

www.ingramcontent.com/pod-product-compliance
Lightning Source LLC
Chambersburg PA
CBHW072047040426
42447CB00012BB/3050